Piano for Singers

Learn to Accompany Yourself and Others

T0082060

CONTENTS

PLAYBACK+

Speed • Pitch • Balance • Loop

To access audio, visit:
www.halleonard.com/mylibrary

Enter Code
2792-1225-1963-2673

ISBN 978-1-4234-5686-5

HAL•LEONARD®

Visit Hal Leonard Online at
www.halleonard.com

World headquarters, contact:
Hal Leonard
7777 West Bluemound Road
Milwaukee, WI 53213
Email: info@halleonard.com

In Europe, contact:
Hal Leonard Europe Limited
1 Red Place
London, W1K 6PL
Email: info@halleonardeurope.com

In Australia, contact:
Hal Leonard Australia Pty. Ltd.
4 Lentara Court
Cheltenham, Victoria, 3192 Australia
Email: info@halleonard.com.au

CHAPTER ONE
SHEET MUSIC AND FORM

Most of us choose the songs we want to sing from songs we hear on recordings and on the radio. But how do we go from hearing a song to singing it and accompanying ourselves? We need a source that will tell us what to play as we sing. And we need an idea of how to begin the song, how to move from section to section, and how to end the song.

SHEET MUSIC: PIANO SCORE, LEAD SHEETS, AND CHARTS

There are two ways to accompany singers: the first is to play what's written on a page, the second is to play what you hear on a recording.

If you have a song on a page, it will be either a **piano score**, a **lead sheet** or a **chart**. With a **piano score**, an entire arrangement of the song is written out, with notes in rhythm, on a set of two staves (plural for "staff") called a **grand staff**. On the grand staff, the treble staff is for the right hand, and the bass staff below it is for the left hand. (We'll cover this in more detail in chapter two.)

1-1

If you want to play all the notes exactly the way they're written, it will take quite a bit of time and effort learning to read music, reading the arrangement on the piano score, and playing it at the right tempo and with the right feel. And it will sound almost exactly the same as when someone else plays it. If you want to take piano lessons and learn to play scales, arpeggios, and classical music so you can read piano scores, by all means, do.

But many musicians who play pop music (that is, rock, jazz, blues, Latin, country, show tunes, etc.) as opposed to classical music, would rather not do this. Some never took piano lessons, and they would struggle to play the piano score. They play "by ear." And some would rather play the song their own way, instead of exactly as the notes are written in the piano score. For them, there are lead sheets and charts.

Lead sheets have the melody of the song written on a treble staff, with the lyrics below the staff and chord symbols above it.

1-2

Charts have chord symbols above the staff, but no melody or lyrics, and only slashes on the staff to indicate where each chord should be played in its measure. (Piano scores sometimes have chord symbols above the treble clef staff, too.) Slash notation will be covered in chapter three.

1-3

If you want to accompany your singing, you can use any of these three printed versions of the song, whichever is more comfortable for you. But we'll be using charts in this book, because it's the easiest way to accompany singing. If you can play a song from a chart, you can play it from the other two, assuming the piano score has chord symbols. Since you're not playing notes on staves, you can play the chords from the chord symbols however you want, anywhere on the keyboard and with the notes in any order. (See "Voicing" in chapter three.)

Once you learn the various ways to play the chord symbols (chapter three), and what rhythm to play them in for each style of music (chapter four), you can play any song from a chart and accompany your singing. And you can decide what ways of playing are most pleasing to you, or easiest, and play your own way. It can be easy, fun, and expressive.

Don't be surprised to see a song written different ways in different books. Music publishers often hire arrangers to set songs differently than the original sheet music. For that reason, a version of a song in one book might have different chords, and even be in a different key, than a version in another book. As you play more, you'll develop your own taste and style, so you can decide not only which arrangement you like better, but also arrange the song the way you like it. (See chapter five.)

Fake books are collections of lead sheets or charts that condense songs into short, easy-to-read versions. A song that may run four or five pages as a piano score can be boiled down to a page-long chart, or even a half-page chart. That way, musicians can carry a book or two to a gig and have hundreds of songs at their fingertips.

If you can't find a printed version of a song you want to sing, you'll have to write a chart for it yourself, by transcribing it from a recording. This takes a lot of practice and good ears. But the more you play, and the more chords you know, the easier it will be to identify the chords being played on the recording, so you can write them into the chart. There will be some exercises in transcribing chords in chapter three. You don't have to play every note the original performer plays. There are, however, transcriptions of many original piano parts, if you're interested.

FORM

Every piece of music has a particular **form:** there are sections of various lengths in a certain order. We give these sections letter names. Most songs have only "A" sections and "B" sections, but some have more.

In pop styles, there are forms that we'll see over and over again. One of the most common is called the Great American Song Form, used in almost every standard written in the first 50 years of the 20th century. A **standard** is a song that has passed from generation to generation, and has been reinterpreted by many artists. Many of the tunes of the great American songwriters of early Broadway, Hollywood, and Tin Pan Alley—like George Gershwin, Cole Porter, and Duke Ellington—are generally thought of as standards.

The Great American Song Form has 32 measures, in four eight-measure sections. The first section, the theme, is called "A." The second section is often a repeat of the theme, so it's another "A." Then the third section is completely different music (the bridge), so it's called "B." Then there's another "A," for a total of 32 bars. A tune that follows this form is "AABA," where the three "A" sections are all the same music (perhaps with slight variations) and the "B" section is different music. Examples of this form include "Satin Doll," "The Lady Is a Tramp," and "As Time Goes By."

The 32 bars can also be ABAC, where there are three different sections of music, all eight bars long. Examples of this form include "Our Love Is Here to Stay," "It Had to Be You," and "Stardust." Both of these forms allow the composer to make his most important musical statement (the "A") and repeat it—so the listener hears it twice and remembers it—but still have something else (that is, "B") in the tune to keep it from being only that statement. The "B" section is often in a different key than the "A" section.

Another popular form is the **12-bar blues**. This consists of one section of 12 measures repeated over and over again. There are many variations on the chords of a 12-bar blues, but it always has three phrases of four bars each. Twelve-bar blues is the most influential form in pop music. You'll hear it in jazz, R&B, rock 'n' roll, and other styles. Examples of this form include "Route 66," "You Ain't Nothin' But a Hound Dog," and "Roll Over Beethoven."

And then there is the **verse-chorus** form used in a lot of folk, country, and rock 'n' roll. The verse, which tells the story, is the "A" section, and the chorus, with the same lyrics every time, is the "B." Songs in these styles often go ABABAB. Examples of this form include "Fire and Rain," "Bad, Bad Leroy Brown," and "Crocodile Rock."

When songwriters wanted to put more variety and interest into their tunes, they began to include more sections of different music. Songs began to have more complex forms, like ABABCAB. Examples include "You've Lost That Lovin' Feelin'," "Piano Man," and "Moondance."

Because music would become stale if it always followed the rules, there are variations on all of these forms. There are standards that have four or eight measures added to the end of their regular 32 bars. There are eight-bar and 16-bar blues tunes. And there are even rock 'n' roll tunes that have only one section repeated over and over again, and songs that have four different sections.

So the singer doesn't have to start singing on the very first beat of the song, there is often an instrumental **introduction** to the song, usually four or eight measures long. A **tag**, a repeat of the last part of the last section, or a short extra section, ends the song in an interesting way. The composers of standards often wrote a longer introduction to their song, with lyrics. This used to be called the **verse**, and the 32-bar form after it was called the **chorus**.

You'll come across other forms, but the ones mentioned above are the most popular. When you read a chart, be aware of the sections going by, and how the form is put together. This will help you recognize repeated patterns, within a song or from one song to another, and play more seamlessly. Chart writers often help you notice the sections by starting and ending each section with a double barline, and by putting rehearsal letters in boxes at the start of each section.

1-4

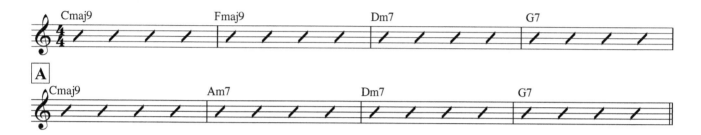

Songs in sheet music versions, especially in charts and lead sheets, often seek to save space on the page by using repeat signs. There are two ways of doing this. The first is to use an open repeat sign at the beginning of the repeated section, and then first and second (and sometimes third) endings, finishing with closed repeat signs, at the end of the repeated section. This is very useful for songs whose sections have very little difference between them, like rock 'n' roll.

Take a look at the sample chart on page 6. It includes repeat signs, rehearsal letters, double bar lines, and chord symbols. The numbers in diamonds are inserted to show you how the tune proceeds from one section to another.

The form of this chart is:

(1) four-measure intro
(2) 16 measures at letter A
(3) 16 measures at letter B, ending with the first ending (4)
(5) 16 measures at letter A again
(6) back to letter B, but only 14 measures this time, skip first ending
(7) second ending

1-5

The second way is to use other symbols to direct the pianist around the page. "D.C." (*da capo*, from the top) means "go back to the very beginning of the tune." "D.S." (*dal segno*, from the sign) means "go back to the big funny S symbol." 𝄋 "To Coda" means "skip down to the end of the chart till you find that crossed circle again." 𝄌

This is very useful for songs whose sections are substantially different—more than just a few measures at the end of a section. You may even see more than one D.S. or Coda in a song, and following the chart can be difficult.

Here is another sample chart that uses D.C., D.S., and Coda. Again, the little numbers in diamonds will show you how the symbols direct you around the page.

The form of this chart is:

(1) four-measure intro
(2) 12 measures at letter A
(3) back to the four-measure intro
(4) 12 more measures of letter A
(5) 12 measures at letter B
(6) back to letter A for ten more measures
(7) skip down to Coda for last four measures

1-6

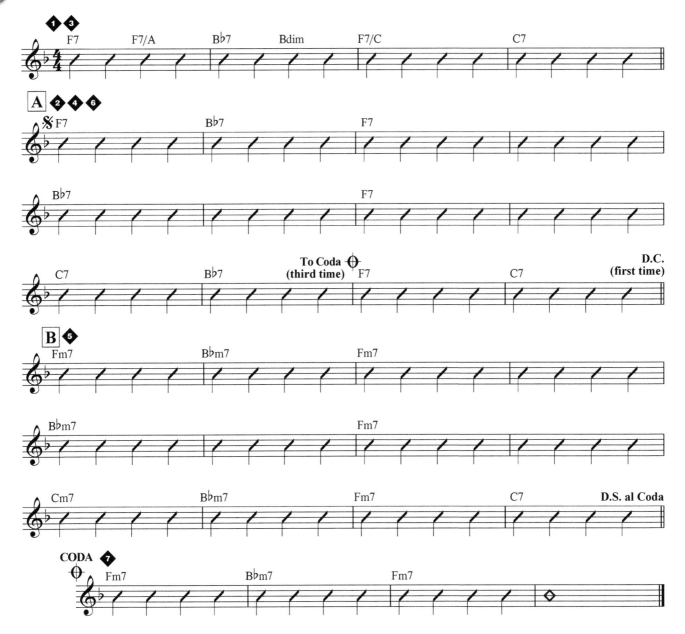

CHAP WRAP

Here's one way of looking at music: like all art forms, music sets up expectations, then either fulfills them or thwarts them. The rules of form, melody, harmony, and rhythm of Western music that have developed over the centuries still apply to much of Western music today. We've heard enough music to be familiar with those rules, whether we know it or not. Standard forms—the Great American Song Form, 12-bar blues, verse-chorus-verse-chorus—fulfill our expectations about how the song will move from section to section, how long each section will be, and how long the song will be. Variations of these forms can surprise us, thwart our expectations. How do you feel when your expectations are fulfilled? How do you feel when they're thwarted? Are you happy when things happen the way you've always heard them happen before, or are you bored? When they don't happen the way you expect them to, are you turned off, or intrigued?

For me, the best music is a healthy balance between elements that do what I expect them to do, so that the song doesn't seem random and confusing, and elements that don't do what I expect them to do, so there's something fresh and exciting to listen to.

CHAPTER TWO
PLAYING MELODIES

THE KEYBOARD

Look at the keys on your piano. You'll notice a pattern: white keys all along the bottom and black keys above them, separated into groups of twos and threes. (Incidentally, the word "key" has two different meanings. Here, it means the note you press on the piano to make a sound. Soon, it will mean something else.) The white key just to the left of each pair of black keys is named C, and the one in the center of the piano is "middle C." The white keys after C are D, E, F, G, A, and B, and then we get to another C and start all over again.

Each key on the piano has a place on the **grand staff**. This is the set of lines that we put notes on, so we can read and play what a composer has written. The grand staff is actually two staves connected by a brace; each staff has five horizontal lines. The notes of the top staff are E above middle C, F, G, A, B, C, D, E, and F again. The notes of the bottom staff are G an octave and a half below middle C, then A, B, C, D, E, F, G, and A again. For notes that are higher or lower than the lines on the staff, we put in extra lines, called ledger lines.

2-1

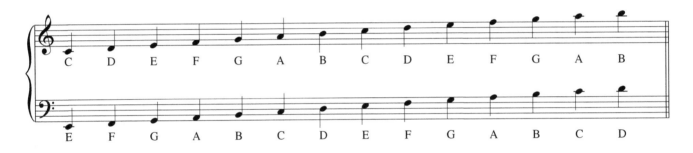

The distance (interval) between each C and the next C above it or below it is called an octave. In fact, the distance or interval between any note and the same note immediately above it or below it is an octave. The letter names of the keys stay the same from octave to octave, but sound different because they're in a different place on the piano.

2-2

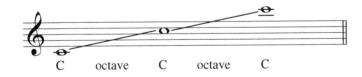

The interval between any key on the piano and the next key immediately above or below it is a half-step. The interval between any note and the note two half-steps above or below it is a whole-step.

2-3

For each interval, indicate whether it is a half-step or a whole-step. (Answers are given on page 60.)

2-4

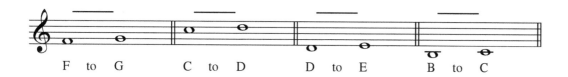

THE MAJOR SCALE

Play the eight white notes from middle C to the C an octave above it. Does that string of notes sound familiar? It's the major scale, which most of us learned in grade school. (We'll get to the minor scale later.)

 2-5

Every song is in a particular key, either major or minor. (Here's the second meaning of the word "key": the system each song is in, determined by the scale it uses.) Every song in the key of C major will primarily use the notes of the C major scale. Sometimes it will use the black notes as well. These five black notes are called **accidentals**—they are outside the key.

Each of these five black notes has two different names; they're called **enharmonic equivalents**. The black note between C and D can be called either "C sharp" (C♯) or "D flat" (D♭), because it is a little higher than C (sharp means higher) and a little lower than D (flat means lower).

Therefore, the note between D and E can be called either "D♯" or "E♭," depending on several different factors, like what key you're in, and what direction the melody is going. Can you tell what two names the note between F and G can be called? And the note between G and A? And the note between A and B?

2-6

Notice that there is no note between E and F, and also no note between B and C.

Because there are 12 different notes (seven in the key; for instance, C, D, E, F, G, A, and B in the key of C major, and five out of the key, the accidentals in C major), there are 12 different keys. Each is just like the one in C, in that it has seven notes in the scale and five out of the scale, and if you play the seven notes in the scale, it will be the major scale again. It will sound very much like the scale you just played, only starting on a different note. Because each scale starts on a different note, it will have different notes in it. No two major scales have the same notes.

To prove this, try playing the eight white keys from F to F. Does it sound like a major scale? One note isn't right. Can you tell which one?

The B isn't right. To make the F major scale, you have to change the B to a B♭, the black key to the left of B. Now play the F major scale with the B♭ in place of the B. Doesn't that sound right? We call this note B♭ and not A♯, because we already have A in the scale, and there can be only one of each letter in each scale. You will never see a scale that has a G and a G♯ in it, or a D and a D♭. There will be one of every letter in the scale, and only one.

Now play all the white keys between G and G. Again, it's not quite a major scale. Play it again and let your ears tell you what needs to be changed. That's right; the F has to be changed to an F♯. Now play the G major scale with an F♯ in place of the F. Doesn't that sound right? So, the sequence of whole-steps and half-steps in any major scale looks like this:

2-7

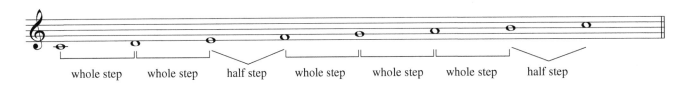

There are many other scales, particularly from music of non-Western countries, but the major scale is the basis for most of Western music.

KEY SIGNATURES

How do we know which notes to play in each scale? The key signature tells us. Right after the clef on the first staff of the song, there is a key signature that tells you what key the song is in. Because there is a B♭ in the F major scale, if you see a flat on the B line in the key signature, you know you're in F. Because there is an F-sharp in the G major scale, if you see a sharp on the F line in the key signature, you know you're in G. The C major scale has no sharps or flats in it, so there are no sharps or flats in its key signature.

Here's a formula for figuring out the key from the key signature:

For sharp keys, find the last sharp and go up a half-step. That's the key.

2-8

For flat keys, find the second-to-last flat. That's the key.

2-8a

Since there is no second-to-last flat in the key of F, you simply have to memorize that one. One flat is the key of F.

What keys are designated by the following key signatures?

2-9

Play the major scales in all 12 keys. Remember, the key signature will tell you what notes to play. Keep your ears open and listen for the correct sound of the major scale.

Since the seven different notes of the major scale change for every key, the five accidentals do, too. If the composer wants to use an accidental in his melody, he has to change the note in the key whenever the accidental occurs.

2-10

Once the note is changed—"accidentalized"—it's changed for the entire measure without another accidental. (A measure ("bar") is the space between vertical barlines on the staff.) But the ending barline cancels out any accidentals from that measure. So if the composer wants to accidentalize that note in the next measure, he has to put another sharp or flat in front of it there.

2-10a

And one more thing before we go on: the minor scale. For every major scale, there's a minor scale related to it called the relative minor. It uses the exact same notes as its relative major cousin, but starting at a different point. The relative minor scale starts on the sixth note of its major cousin, so the minor scale related to C major is A minor. That natural minor scale is A B C D E F G and A again, because those are the notes used in the C major scale. Using A minor as an example, here is the sequence of whole-steps and half-steps found in any natural minor scale:

2-11

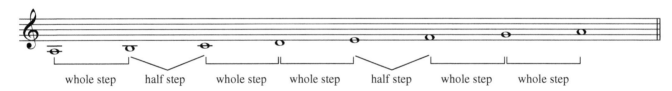

There are variations on this minor scale. But play the notes as written, and when you're in a minor key, you'll hear how it differs from a melody in a major key. We'll have more on relative minors in chapter three.

MELODIES

So now you know the names of each key on the piano, and how to tell which of the keys is called for on the staff. Play the following strings of notes, and don't worry about the rhythm. Just play them when you find them.

 2-12

The more you play, the more you'll be able to take your eyes off the keys. This is important, because it will make reading easier. Eventually, when you don't need to read any longer, it will make performing easier. You'll have a picture of the keyboard in your head, and your hands will also have a memory of where the keys are, so you can find them without looking, and concentrate on singing. Keep your ears open while you're focusing so much energy through your eyes. The more you hear, the more the things you see will make sense. The piano doesn't play itself, but with enough practice, you won't have to think so hard. Your body will remember how to play what it has played many times before.

As you play, the words of the old piano teacher will be ringing in your ears: "Sit up straight, relax, and curve your fingers." These are good ideas, because they make playing easier. Try to develop good playing habits, and they'll pay off in the long run.

You may wonder which fingers to use with which keys. Obviously it will be easier and you'll be able to play more quickly if you use all five fingers, instead of trying to play the keys with only one finger (like "hunting and pecking" on a computer keyboard). There are many books that can teach you the best fingering for each scale, and for other things like arpeggios (the notes in a chord played one after another). But for our purposes, start with your thumb or pinky and go up or down the keyboard with the other fingers in order. Correct fingering isn't important now; you're just learning to plunk out melodies.

Incidentally, there are pedals at your feet. The one on the right sustains the sound you've just made. Try playing something without pressing it down, and then the same thing with it pressed down. The one on the left makes what you play quieter. Again, try playing with, then without. As for the pedal in the middle... no one knows what that one does.

RHYTHM AND TIME SIGNATURES

Now it's time to play melodies in rhythm. Every song has a certain **time signature**, right after the key signature on the first staff. It has two numerals, like a fraction. The top one indicates how many beats there are in a measure; the bottom one indicates what type of note gets one beat. In 4/4, there are four beats in each measure, and each beat is equal to a quarter-note. That doesn't mean there are always four quarter-notes in every measure. There can be two half-notes or one whole-note or eight eighth-notes or sixteen 16th-notes or any combination of these that equals four quarter-notes. Sometimes, 4/4 is replaced by a capital C in the time signature; they mean the same thing.

2-13

Here's how to count your way through a measure of 4/4: use the numbers 1-2-3-4 for all the beats, and the word "and" for the eighth-notes between the beats. When there are 16th-notes, use "ee" for the ones before the eighth-notes, and "ah" for the ones after the eighth-notes:

2-14

Which of these measures has the correct number of beats?

2-15

Cut-time is 4/4's cousin. It's written the same way and read the same way. There are still four quarter-notes' worth of music in each measure, but it's felt and counted differently. It's actually 2/2, meaning that there are only two beats per measure, and the half-note gets one beat. So if you have a measure in cut-time that has four quarter-notes in it, you would count "1-&-2-&" instead of "1-2-3-4." It can be notated as 2/2 or as a capital C with a vertical slash through it.

2-16

The difference between 4/4 and cut-time is very subtle, and you may not know which time signature is being used in a song just by listening to it. But the instruments accompanying your singing will play 4/4 differently from cut-time.

In 3/4, there is three quarter-notes' worth of music in each measure. Waltzes are in 3/4. Which of these measures has the correct number of beats?

2-17

In 6/8, there are six beats to the measure and the eighth-note gets one beat. Which of these measures has the correct number of beats?

2-18

Now play the same set of notes you played earlier, but play them in the correct rhythm, in time. Set a tempo in your head—the correct number of beats going by in each measure at an even, regular pace—and align the notes to those beats.

Now try playing these exercises.

 2-19

Sometimes the composer wants to stop the melody for a while. He uses **rests** for this. There's a rest for every kind of note, and when you see a rest of a certain time value, you stop singing or playing for that amount of time, that number of beats, before beginning again.

2-20

whole rest   half rest   quarter rest   eighth rest   16th rest

Dots after notes or rests extend the value of those notes or rests by one-half.

2-21

Ties link one note to another on the same space or line, extending the first note's value.

2-22

Triplets are sets of three notes that fit into the space usually taken up by two notes. Three eighth-note triplets fit into the space where two eighth-notes usually go. Three quarter-note triplets fit into the space where two quarter-notes usually go. And three half-note triplets fit into the space where two half-notes usually go.

 2-23

Simple music, and often older music, puts an emphasis, an accent (>), on the first and third beats of every measure of 4/4. **Syncopation**, a big part of relatively modern music, puts the accent on a note that is off the beat, often the "and" between the numbers.

 2-24

Syncopation can be rather simple, or incredibly complicated. You have to count your way through the measure very carefully.

Here are some exercises for playing melodies. They contain notes and rests, dots and ties, and some simple syncopation.

2-25

When you play melodies, keep your ears open for patterns. Melodies often repeat sections, or set a pattern and then vary it. That's how composers make melodies memorable, so they'll stay in our heads. One particular pattern is called a **sequence**. That's when the composer writes one bit of the melody in one part of the scale, and then repeats it in another part.

2-26

Now that you can play melodies, you can learn songs by yourself, and teach others. In order to accompany yourself or others, you have to learn to play harmony (chapter three) and play in various styles (chapter four).

When you get to the next chapter, you'll have to read a little bit of bass clef. Here again are the notes you'll use most often:

2-27

Lastly, don't spend so much time trying to get all the notes right that you lose your sense of musicianship. This applies to what you learn in the next two chapters as well. Listen to what you're playing. Evaluate it, change it. What sounds good to you? Since you're not playing the piano score, note for note as written, you get to be artistic and creative. Get your eyes out of the music and off the keyboard as soon as you can, keep your ears open, and make music!

CHAP WRAP

Simple melodies, like the ones we often hear in children's songs, holiday songs, and folk music, go up and down the scale, repeat notes, repeat patterns, avoid accidentals, and limit big intervals. That way, they're easy to sing. We all get used to these melodies early in life. Then, music in more complicated styles—like classical, jazz, and Broadway show tunes—surprises us with accidentals and intervals we're not used to. The melodies are harder to sing. But with greater complexity can come greater expression, greater subtlety, and greater variety. The more you listen, the more you'll get used to, understand, and appreciate complexity.

CHAPTER THREE
HARMONY

TRIADS OF THE CONFIGURATION

Harmony is the notes that accompany the melody. Harmony in music of the Western world is based on **chords**, and the rules developed over the centuries have determined how those chords are formed and how they most often move from one to another.

Chords are groups of notes that are played simultaneously, usually three or more at a time. **Triads** are chords that have three notes, called 1 (or the root), 3, and 5, each the interval of a third apart. This interval of a third can either be a major third (M3, which is four half-steps on the piano), or a minor third (m3, which is only three half-steps).

If you create triads out of the notes of the scale of whatever key your music is in, those chords will look like snowmen walking up a hill. This is what I call The Configuration. Here's The Configuration in the key of C:

 3-1

These triads are the building blocks of harmony. You'll use them, and variations of them, all the time, in every style of music. Play these chords, using the thumb, middle finger, and pinky of your right hand.

We give each of these chords a Roman numeral name and a chord symbol. No matter what key you're in, the Roman numerals are always the same. But the chord symbols change with each key. They tell you specifically what chord to play.

Let's put the two sets of names above The Configuration:

3-2

Play these chords while you say their names. From now on when you play something on the piano, look at the shape it makes. Is it a straight line across the keyboard? Is it a triangle? If so, is the triangle pointing up or down? These shapes will help you remember how to play. And keep your ears open, too. Try to memorize the sound of what you're playing. What does a major triad sound like? What does a minor triad sound like? Keep listening to what you play, and ask yourself, "Does that sound right?"

FIVE MAJOR KEYS

The keys that you will come across most often in songs of every style are C, F, G, B♭, and E♭. If you can play the important chords in each of these keys, you can play a lot of songs in a lot of styles. Here are The Configurations for three of the remaining four keys with Roman numeral and letter names for their triads:

3-3

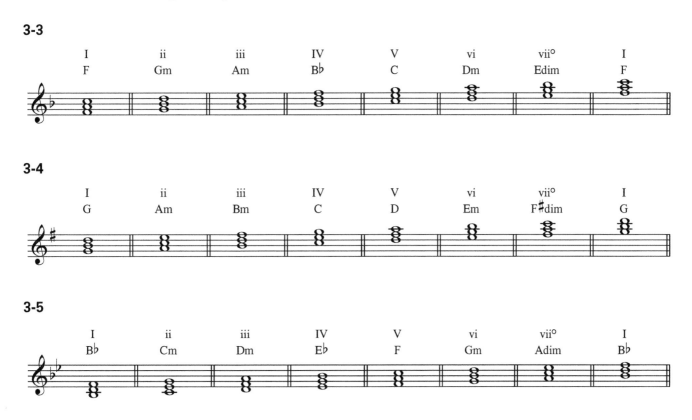

Now write The Configuration for the last key, E♭:

3-6

Notice that in every key, the Roman numerals are exactly the same. Some are capital letters (major chords, where the 3 is a M3 above the root) and some are small letters (minor chords, where the 3 is a m3 above the root). The other chord has "dim" after it. That's the abbreviation for "diminished." The diminished chord has a minor third, and unlike any of the other chords, it also has a diminished or lowered fifth. Note: often the diminished chord is abbreviated with a raised or superscripted "o" instead of "dim;" I prefer the former.

Play all the chords in these five Configurations while you say their names. Make sure you're playing the notes in the key signature. Can you hear how the major chords sound major and the minor chords sound minor? Can you hear the unusual quality of the only diminished chord in each Configuration? Can you hear how all the Configurations sound similar, because they all have the same types of chords in the same order? Only the pitches are different.

If you have to play in another key, write out The Configuration in that key and play those chords.

THE RELATIVE MINOR KEYS

As we learned in chapter two, every major key—like the ones we've written Configurations for so far—has a minor key related to it. This is called the **relative minor** because it uses the same chords as its major cousin. The notes of the two scales are exactly the same, but they start in different places. Here are the relative minor Configurations for our first three keys, with their names:

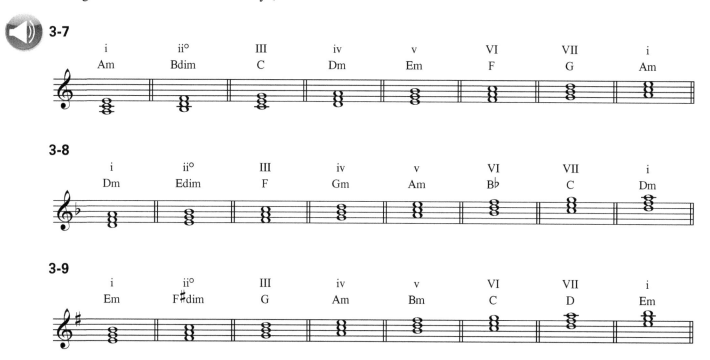

Now write them for the last two keys:

3-10

3-11

Notice two things about relative minor Configurations:

1) The Roman numerals have been shifted over: the minor triads are now i, iv, and v, the major triads are now III, VI, and VII, and the diminished triad is now ii;

2) The relative minor key has the same key signature as its major relative.

Now play them while you say their two names. Can you still hear the major triads, the minor triads, and the diminished triads?

SEVENTH CHORDS

If all music were made up of nothing but triads, music would be very boring. We can add notes to the triads to make them more interesting. If we add one more snowball to the top of the snowmen in the Configurations (again a M3 or m3 above), we'll have **seventh chords**:

3-12

There are four types of seventh chords:

1) Imaj7 and IVmaj7 are **major** seventh chords, because they are **major triads** with 7s a M3 up from their 5s. Play them as you say their names (use thumb, second, third, and fifth fingers).

2) ii7, iii7 and vi7 are **minor** seventh chords, because they are minor triads with 7s a m3 up from their 5s. Play them as you say their names.

3) V7 is the only chord in The Configuration that we call a dominant seventh; it's a major triad with its 7 a m3 up from its 5. Play it as you say its name.

4) vii°7 is the only chord in The Configuration that we call a half-diminshed seventh; it's a diminished triad with its 7 a M3 up from its 5. Play it as you say its name. This chord can either be labelled with an "o" with a slash through it, which I prefer, or as min7♭5. There is another diminished chord that we'll get to later.

Now write out the Configuration of seventh chords in the four other major keys we've had, and in A minor:

3-13

3-14

3-15

3-16

3-17

Play all these Configurations while saying the names of the chords in them. Be careful to play the notes that are in the key signatures.

MAJOR 6TH CHORDS AND MINOR 6TH CHORDS

Just like the various seventh chords, adding the note a major sixth above the root makes a new, more interesting chord out of the original triad:

3-18

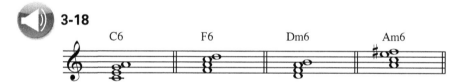

Play the maj6 and min6 chords on every note in the five major scales.

NINTH CHORDS

If we add one more note to each snowman, we get **ninth chords**. There are several different ones that get used all the time, in many styles of music:

3-19

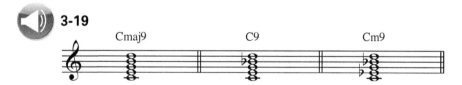

Add the note a M9 above the root to any maj7, min7, or 7 chord and you'll get one of these ninth chords.

There are also two other ninth chords that are used primarily in blues, rock, and—especially—jazz music:

3-20

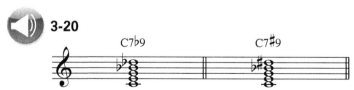

Play all these ninth chords while saying their names. Try to memorize their sounds. Play them starting on different notes.

AUGMENTED CHORDS, FULLY-DIMINISHED CHORDS, AND SUSPENDED CHORDS

There are three other important chords that you'll see, particularly in jazz: the **augmented chord**, whose symbol is a plus sign (+); the **fully-diminished chord**, which is labeled with a circle, like a degree sign and a "7;" and the **suspended chord**, abbreviated "sus." Here are two examples of each. Play them.

3-21

The augmented chord is a major triad with its 5 raised by one half-step; the fully-diminished chord is a diminished triad with its 7 lowered by one whole-step; and the suspended chord is a triad with its 3 raised by one half-step (to 4). These chords put more flavor into harmony, and now when you see them you'll know how to play them

Now try writing the following chords:

3-22

You now have a large vocabulary of chords. If you want to get a fuller sense of what a song sounds like while you're learning it, you can play the melody in the right hand while playing these chords in the left, as close together as possible on the keyboard. If you play the chords too low, they'll sound muddy. Try to play them in the two octaves surrounding middle C.

INVERSIONS

There are also different ways of playing the chords you've already learned. If you want something more interesting, play one of the other notes of the chord in the left hand. This is called an **inversion**, and its chord symbol looks like a fraction. The symbol to the left of the slash is the chord you're familiar with, but the note to the right of the slash is the note you play in the bass with your left hand.

3-23

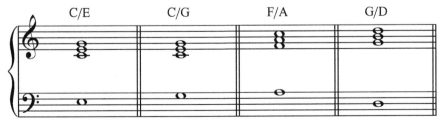

Say the names of these four chords while you play them. Now play these four chords and figure out what their chord symbols are.

3-24

FRACTIONS

Fractions are chords that have a note other than the root of the chord in the left hand. We just saw some of them in inversions. But there are also chords whose left-hand note isn't in the right-hand chord at all. These are often used in pop music:

 3-25

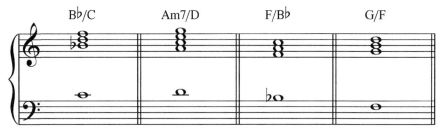

VOICING

So far, all the chords you've been playing in your right hand have been in **root position**, meaning the root (or the 1) is the lowest note of the chord. And so far you've been playing other notes of the chord in order after that, with the 3 above the 1 and the 5 above the 3. But you don't have to play them that way, and you might prefer a different sound. Remember, because you're not playing specific notes from a piano score, you can play the chords indicated by the chord symbols however you want, with the notes in any order, and anywhere on the keyboard. As long as all the notes in the chord are represented somehow, you can choose where to put them.

It's often easier to play the chords in other ways. Here's a progression of chords, all in root position:

3-26

It's fine if you play them like that. But you'll have to move your right hand quite a bit to play everything in root position. Isn't it easier to play the chords in a different voicing, with inversions?

3-27

There are three ways of playing every three-part chord: **root position** (with 1 at the bottom), **first inversion** (with 3 at the bottom), and **second inversion** (with 5 at the bottom). There's a fourth way of playing every four-part chord: **third inversion** (with the 6 or 7 on the bottom). This principle also applies to chords with more notes in them.

3-28

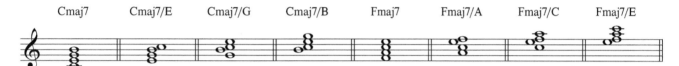

Now, practice playing each of the chords you've learned in each of its inversions. Look at the keyboard as you play them, and take in their shapes. That will help you to play them without looking. Also, listen while you play them, and take in their sounds. That will help you to identify them when you hear them.

Finally, name the following chords:

3-29

Until now, with only triads, all of our chords have been **consonant**, meaning they don't contain two notes that are close enough to each other to create **dissonance**. Dissonance is the sound made by two notes very close together on the keyboard, a half-step or whole-step apart. As you play these four-part chords, particularly in their inversions, you'll hear dissonance. Do you like the sound?

TRANSPOSITION

If a song is printed or recorded in a key that is either too high or too low for you, you may want to put it in a more comfortable key. This is called **transposition**, and it's important not only for singers, but also for teachers who have students with ranges other than the "standard" range.

Think of transposition as a puzzle: if the first chord of the song is this chord in the original key, what does it have to be in the new key? Once you've found the answer, you can play that new chord wherever the old chord appears in the original. And then you go on to the next chord and the next, until all the chords are transposed. Imagine trying to transpose all the notes in a piano score. No wonder pianists who don't play from charts never want to transpose.

Here's something very important about transposing. There are two parts to every chord: the letter name (the note of the scale that the chord is built on), and the type of chord. It's the letter name of the chord that you want to transpose, not the type of chord. For example, if the chord is a maj7 in the original, make sure that it's a maj7 in the transposition.

Here are some examples of transposition:

3-30

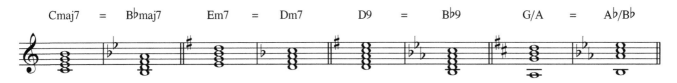

Transpose the following chords to the new keys indicated by the new key signatures:

3-31

And finally, here is a short song for you to transpose:

3-32

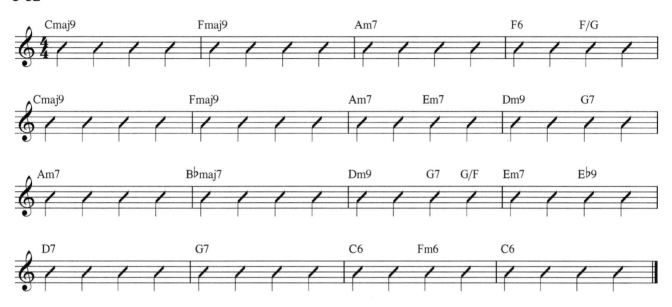

becomes:

3-33

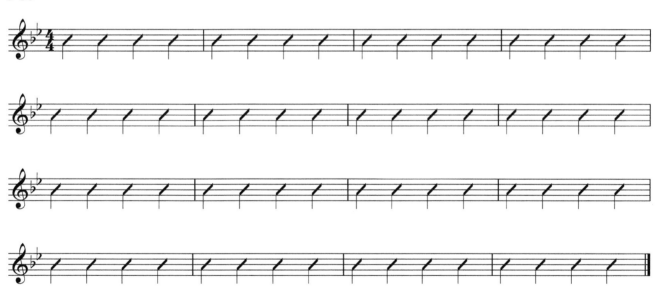

Note that we've started using slash notation. If there are no particular rhythms you want to notate—that is, if everything moves along as expected, four quarter-notes to the measure and chords changing mostly on downbeats—you can simply use slashes like this:

3-34

If you want to notate a more particular rhythm, like you would with notes and rests, use the following :

3-35

HARMONIC TRANSCRIPTION

If you are unable to find a printed source of any kind for a song you want to sing, you'll have to figure out the chords from listening to a recording. This is called **harmonic transcription**. It takes a lot of practice and can be very involved, more involved than we'll get to in this book. Again, the more you play and keep your ears open, the more you'll recognize chords and the **progressions** they often fall into. (Progressions are groups of chords that make a harmonic phrase.)

Here are a few tips for transcribing harmony:

1. Lay out the chart. Figure out how many sections there are, how many measures there are in each section, and make room for them on the paper. That way, you'll know where to put the chords when you identify them. Try to get four measures on each line of the staff, and fit the entire song on one page if possible. Put in the repeats, double bar lines, rehearsal letters, and time signature. Write in pencil first, so you can correct mistakes. When you're all done, ink everything and erase the pencil.

2. Determine the key the song is in, put in the key signature, and write the chords in that key. Then if you need to check something on the piano, you can check it against the recording. If the key isn't right for you, you can transpose it later. How do you determine the key? Find the I chord (called the **tonic** chord) where the song feels finished or resolved. The first chord of the song is usually the tonic, and the last chord of the song is almost always the tonic.

3. Listen to the bass. Most styles of music have the bass playing roots of chords more often than not. If you can hear the bass note whenever the chord changes, you'll know at least the letter name of the chord. But be careful: some styles have more active bass parts that play a lot more notes than just the roots of the chords. Try to hear the bass notes on the downbeats of measures, and other places where the chords change.

4. After you've got letter names for the chords from the bass notes, determine the types of chords. Major or minor? Seventh, maj7, min7? Diminished, augmented, suspended? Fraction? If you can't recognize the type of chord, sing along with the song and when you get to that chord, stop the recording and try to play the notes you can still hear. Play three or four correct notes and you'll have your chord.

5) Listen for standard progressions such as 12-bar blues and others that you find in many tunes.

Here are four exercises for you to transcribe:

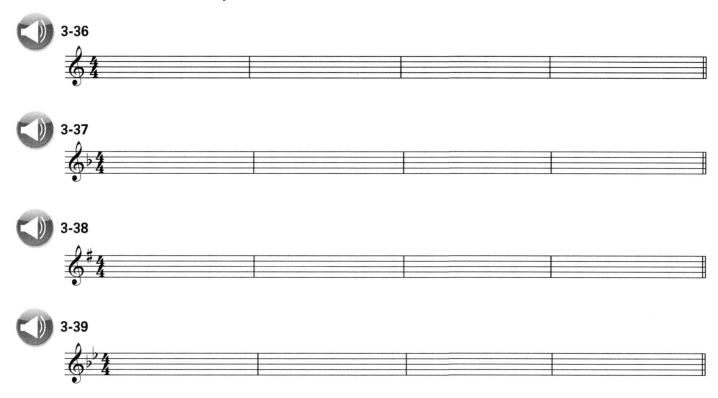

3-36

3-37

3-38

3-39

Here is a song for you to transcribe:

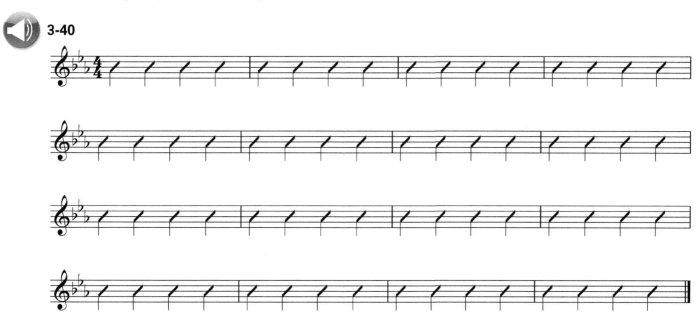

3-40

CHAP WRAP

Simple harmonies—triads in The Configuration, standard progressions—fulfill our youthful expectations. More complicated music introduces chords outside The Configuration, four- and five-note chords, augmented and diminished chords, fractions, dissonance, unusual progressions, and even substitutes other chords for the ones we're used to hearing. These more complicated harmonies can add drama to music, warmth, subtlety, rich emotion. They can also be so dissonant or so unusual that they disobey the rules of Western music's harmony to the point that they offend our ears. Complex harmony is often an acquired taste. The more you listen to music of different styles, the more you'll appreciate it.

CHAPTER FOUR
STYLES

Now that you know how to play most of the chords you'll encounter as you read charts, the next step is to play them in a particular style. A set of chords by itself doesn't necessarily dictate what style to play. Any set of chords can be played in several different styles. You've learned the "what." Now it's time for the "how."

Essentially, playing different styles means playing chords in particular rhythmic patterns. This is one of the most important things that makes a song Latin or jazz or rock 'n' roll. And since some of the other things that determine style may be dependent on other instruments (a slide guitar in country-western, a fiddle in bluegrass) or the way you sing the song (lots of licks in R&B, scat in jazz), the rhythmic patterns you play on the piano largely determine the particular style.

For basic accompaniment, you'll need to learn only one rhythmic pattern for each style, and use it continually throughout the tune. You don't need to change patterns from measure to measure, or even from section to section. Oftentimes, when you're accompanying yourself, simpler is better. But as you increase your ability, you may want to change patterns, especially from section to section, to give your song more variety.

So in this chapter, you'll learn a basic accompaniment pattern for each of many different styles of music, and then often a spicier one. You'll then use those patterns to play samples in those styles. You'll pick out the melodies from those samples, learn them, and then accompany yourself singing them using the patterns. Finally, there will be a short list of songs that you can play using the patterns for each style. To find the music for most of those songs, I suggest the following fake books, published by Hal Leonard:

The Ultimate Jazz Fakebook (HL00240079)
The Real Book (HL00240221)
The New Broadway Fakebook (HL00138905)
The Ultimate Pop/Rock Fakebook (HL00240099)
The Ultimate Country Fakebook (HL00240049)

One more thing about style before we start: sometimes it can be difficult to identify a style. We may be able to recognize jazz when we hear it—although there are many different types of jazz—but can we tell rock 'n' roll from R&B? Blues from R&B? Sometimes the differences are subtle, and there can be a lot of overlap. What style of music did the Beatles play? What about Ray Charles? And James Taylor? The lines can blur.

BALLADS

Here's a pattern that can be used on almost every style of 4/4 ballad, if it's **straight** as opposed to **swung**. (We'll get to swing in a little bit.) The right hand plays four quarter-note chords per measure, very evenly. The left hand plays two roots of the chord, an octave apart, in the rhythm shown below. Play the right hand first, then the left, then put them together. Use your thumb, index finger, and pinky in the right hand; use the thumb and pinky for the two notes in the left hand.

4-1

Change the chords in the right hand, usually on 1 and 3 of each measure, and change the roots in the left hand accordingly:

4-2

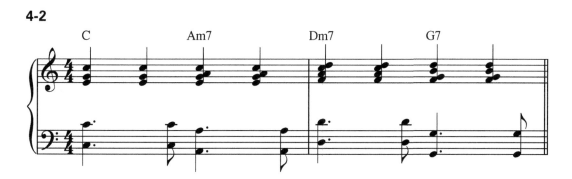

Learn the melody to this sample, then use this pattern to accompany yourself singing it. Play the chords in the octaves above middle C, and the bass notes in the octaves below middle C. Change octaves when you need to, or if you like a particular sound. Work on the accompaniment until you can get it steady enough to sing over without breaking the rhythm. Don't worry if you take it very slowly at first.

 4-3

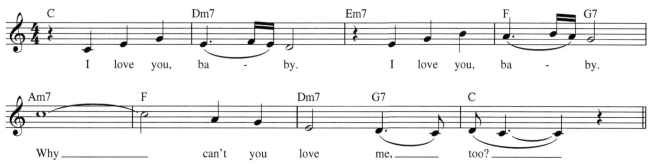

Here is a way to vary this pattern so it will be a little more interesting:

4-4

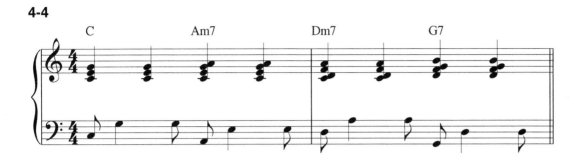

For ballads in cut-time (2/2), each measure should have half as many notes: play one whole-note in the left hand instead of two half-notes, and two half-notes in the right hand instead of four quarter-notes.

As soon as you can, memorize the chords, so you can take your eyes off of them, refer to the lyrics or melody if you need to, and look at the keyboard as necessary. Your eyes can do only so much at one time; the more you memorize, the less they'll have to do.

Now use the basic 4/4 ballad pattern to play these tunes:

"Misty"
"On the Street Where You Live"
"There's a Place for Us"
"Over the Rainbow"
"If I Loved You"
"Imagine"
"My Funny Valentine"
"Bridge Over Troubled Water"
"All Out of Love"

Use these patterns for straight ballads in pop, rock, country, contemporary Christian, Broadway, jazz and standards, and especially for simple children's songs, Christmas carols, and folk songs.

There is a difference between **straight ballads** (usually rock, country, show tunes) and **swing ballads** (often jazz, blues, and R&B). Swing ballads have a slightly bouncier rhythm. Some of the eighth-notes are in slightly different places in the measure. In straight rhythms, eighth-notes last the same amount of time and look like this:

4-5

1 & 2 & 3 & 4 & 1 & 2 & 3 & 4 &

In swing rhythm, they look like this:

4-6

1   ah   2   ah   3   ah   4   ah   1   ah   2   ah   3   ah   4   ah

or this:

4-7

trip - let trip - let trip - let trip - let   trip - let trip - let trip - let trip - let

Because this would be a lot to write into every chart, arrangers often simply indicate "Swing" in the top left corner of the chart and/or state these designations to indicate that the song should be swung throughout:

4-8

 4-9

Listen to the difference between a straight rhythm and a swing rhythm.

Play this pattern, which swings the left hand:

4-10

Now try this rhythm, which swings the right hand:

4-11

You now have two swing ballad patterns that can be used on these songs:

"Since I Fell for You"
"Georgia on My Mind"
"The Nearness of You"

Here's a pattern that can be very useful on rock ballads, especially ones from the early rock era. It can be written two different ways: either you stay in 4/4 and play four sets of triplets in each measure in the right hand, or you change the time signature to 12/8, with 12 eighth-notes per measure:

4-12

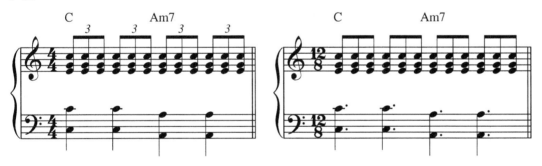

In both cases, play roots in the left hand on each beat. Try this pattern over the following sample:

 4-13

Ba - by, won't you be my lit-tle ba - by? Please? _____

Now that you've learned it, try it on these songs:

"Blueberry Hill"
"I Can't Help Falling in Love with You"
"Unchained Melody"

So far, you've been playing two roots in the left hand. But eventually you can play 1 and 5 in the left hand, or 1, 5, and 7. Eventually, you can drop the "1" note from the chords in the right hand, when you play two roots (the "1" of the chord) in the left hand.

WALTZES

Now we turn to 3/4, waltz time. Some of our greatest show tunes and standards are waltzes, and some country tunes as well. But 3/4 can sound sort of old-fashioned, so it's not used very much anymore. Here's an easy way to play it:

4-14

Use this pattern on the following sample:

4-15

Now use it to play these songs:

"Always"
"Falling in Love with Love"
"Tennessee Waltz"
"Edelweiss"
"Sunrise, Sunset"

Even if you want to play an up-tempo waltz, you can use this pattern. Just speed up the tempo. Here is a pattern you can use on more modern waltzes:

4-16

Use this on tunes like "Weekend in New England" and "What the World Needs Now Is Love."

There is also a jazz waltz. As with most things in jazz, it's more complicated. Try this pattern:

4-17

Try playing the songs listed above as jazz waltzes. You can also try making waltzes or jazz waltzes out of tunes that were originally in 4/4. Each measure of 4/4 becomes two measures of 3/4.

BROADWAY SHOW TUNES

Show tunes from Broadway musicals have been written in many different styles. There are standard ballads and waltzes and Latin tunes, stride and walking bass jazz tunes, as well as rock (*Hair*) and even country (*Big River*). Learn all these styles and you'll be able to play most show tunes. But there is another pattern that Broadway composers have used, often for its most dramatic ballads and anthems:

4-18

Although this pattern can be found in other styles, some of the most famous showstoppers in Broadway history can be played with it. Try it on this sample:

4-19

Now try it on the following tunes:

"You'll Never Walk Alone"
"Memory"
"The Impossible Dream"

Although Broadway up-tempos come from shows of many different musical styles—and you'll be able to use the patterns you're about to learn in order to play them—here's another pattern that's often used in musicals:

4-20

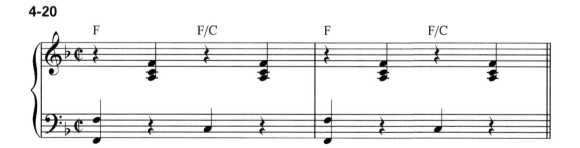

Try it on the following sample:

 4-21

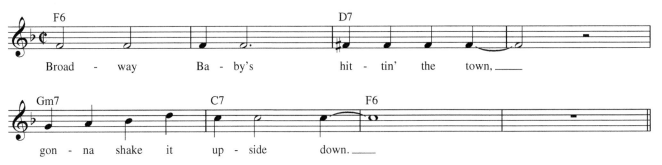

And use it on the following tunes:

"Guys and Dolls"
"There Is Nothing Like a Dame"
"Do-Re-Mi"

COUNTRY

Country up-tempos are often a combination of folk, blues, and rock 'n' roll. Here's a country shuffle that makes use of rocking octaves in the left hand. You'll use this rocking bass pattern in rock 'n' roll and R&B, too. That's why you've been playing octave roots in the left hand.

 4-22

Here's a sample:

 4-23

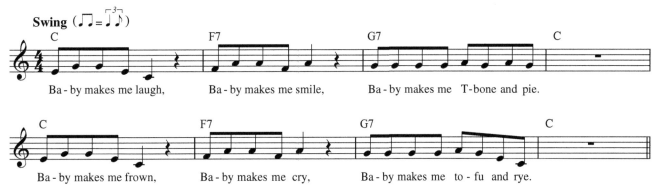

Try this pattern on these tunes:

"Behind Closed Doors"
"Forever and Ever, Amen"
"Friends in Low Places"

BLUES, R&B, AND ROCK 'N' ROLL

Blues is the most influential style of music in the 20th century. Many other styles came out of it—jazz, R&B, rock 'n' roll ("The blues had a baby and they called it rock 'n' roll."), and then soul and funk. There are different kinds of blues, but most of them have the familiar 12-bar pattern. Traditionally, blues tunes are slow and mournful. But they can be happy, too, and even funny. Listen to Bessie Smith, B.B. King, Muddy Waters, Buddy Guy, Stevie Ray Vaughan, and Koko Taylor.

Here's a basic blues pattern:

4-24

Try it on this sample:

4-25

R&B took the blues tunes that jazz bands were playing and added bounce to them. Originally it was called "jump swing." (Listen to Louis Jordan, and count the 12-bar patterns going by.) But R&B got more refined, changed names, and gave us great artists like Aretha Franklin, Marvin Gaye, Al Green, the Temptations, and James Brown.

Rock 'n' roll combined R&B with country. Early rockers like Elvis Presley and Jerry Lee Lewis were thought of as country crossover artists. Then the Beatles and the Rolling Stones made rock their own, and Elton John and Billy Joel continued the evolution.

We've already had some patterns for rock ballads. Let's turn to up-tempo rock tunes. Because rock usually relies heavily on guitars, your piano accompaniment should try to imitate guitar patterns as much as possible. Here's a very popular rock 'n' roll pattern:

4-26

Keep the left hand playing this pattern, change it for each chord, and syncopate the right hand.

Here's a version that's a little spicier. At any tempo, it takes a lot of muscle in your left arm to get through an entire tune with this pattern. Try to relax your shoulder and arm as much as possible. You may want to save this pattern for the end of the tune when it will have more power.

4-27

Try it on this sample:

4-28

Now play it on these songs:

"Jailhouse Rock"
"Johnny B. Goode"
"Old Time Rock & Roll"

Sometimes rock 'n' roll plays straight eighths with this pattern. Sometimes it uses swing eighths, as do the blues and R&B. Try to swing these tunes:

"Blue Suede Shoes"
"Sweet Home Chicago"
"Your Mama Don't Dance"

Here's another pattern for rock 'n' roll up-tempos:

4-29

Try this pattern on the following sample:

4-30

Ba-by with the red dress on, gon-na write you a rock-in' song.

Gon-na play it ev-'ry night and day. __ Ba-by, stay with me. __

Try it on the following tunes:

"Under the Boardwalk"
"Breaking Up Is Hard to Do"
"My Life"

Now for some R&B:

4-31

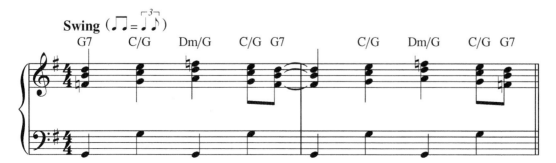

Try this pattern on the following sample:

4-32

Try it on the following tunes:

"The Way You Do the Things You Do"
"Gimme Some Lovin'"
"Get Ready"

And here's a spicier pattern:

4-33

You can use this pattern on the following songs:

"Shop Around"
"I Second That Emotion"
"Dancing in the Streets"

JAZZ AND STANDARDS

Let's turn to jazz and standard up-tempos. Songs of many styles can be considered standards, but for the most part we're talking about songs written in the first 50 years of the 20th century, for musicals (Broadway or film), and for the radio. As stated earlier, the great songs of George Gershwin, Cole Porter, Irving Berlin, Richard Rodgers, and their contemporaries qualify.

Jazz players have taken these songs and others and made them jazz tunes by the way they've played them: with swing rhythms, improvisation, and harmonic substitutions. Now we're talking Benny Goodman, Tommy Dorsey, and Art Tatum. But they've also written their own great jazz tunes, not taken from other souces, like "Round Midnight," "Night in Tunisia," and "Ornithology." Now we're talking about Charlie Parker, Dizzy Gillespie, and Thelonious Monk.

One pattern that can provide a lot of energy on these tunes is called **stride**. Essentially, it's playing a very regular pattern on the beats in the left hand, while syncopating chords in the right hand.

4-34

Again, work the hands separately, then put them together. This can be like patting your head and rubbing your stomach at the same time. But practice enough and it will begin to feel natural. Use it on the following sample:

4-35

Use this pattern on the following tunes:

"It Had to Be You"
"Just in Time"
"All of Me"

Another pattern that can generate a lot of excitement is the walking bass. This is what the bass player often does on jazz tunes and standards, so listen to the bass on recordings of these tunes, and try to play with your left hand what the bass is playing. There are lots of variations, but here's the basic idea: play the notes of the scale on which the chord is built, on even quarter-notes. If the chords change on the downbeats of every measure, you have four notes to play. Try 1, 2, 3, and 5 of the scale ("walking up" the scale) or 1, 7, 6, and 5 ("walking down" the scale):

4-36

1-2-3-5 works well with major chords, while 1-2-3-♯3 works well with minor chords.

If the chords change every two measures, you have eight notes to play, so you can put two of these patterns together:

4-37

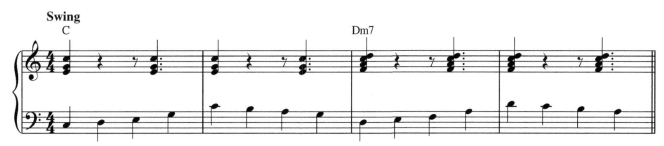

Then the chord changes and you play one of those patterns based on the new scale. Eventually you will be able to think ahead and play a pattern that puts your hand in a good position to play the next one. Here's a sample:

4-38

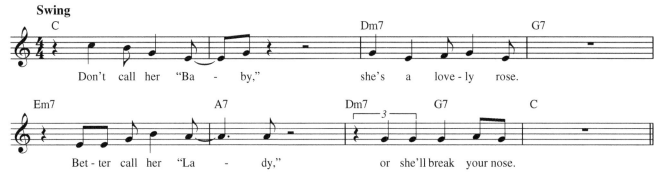

Try this on the following tunes:

"The Lady Is a Tramp"
"Fly Me to the Moon"
"I Get a Kick Out of You"

Walking bass can get very complicated and good bass players can play much more interesting patterns. But for now, these simple ones will get you through a lot of swing tunes.

LATIN

Just as the ballad waltz and the up-tempo waltz can be played with the same pattern, so can the Latin ballad and the Latin up-tempo. There are many types of Latin rhythms— cha-cha, beguine, tango, rhumba, and others. Here's a basic rhythm that works well on Latin tunes (like the great songs of Brazil's Antonio Carlos Jobim) and on American songs that have adopted Latin flavor (like some of Cole Porter's greatest), and any others you want to try:

4-39

Notice how syncopated the right hand is. The aim is to play a lot of syncopation in the right hand while maintaining a steady even rhythm in the left hand. Play each hand separately, then put them together. Try this pattern on the following sample:

4-40

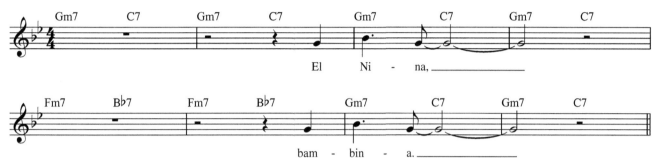

Now try it on these Latin tunes:

"The Girl from Ipanema"
"A Day in the Life of a Fool"
"How Insensitive"

And on these standards:

"Night and Day"
"I've Got You Under My Skin"
"Green Dolphin Street"

Now here's something a little spicier:

4-41

CHAP WRAP

Each genre of music has certain instruments, rhythms, and vocal styles associated with it. Bluegrass has a fiddle, Latin music has congas, country has slide guitar, R&B has singers with great licks. Those elements fulfill our expectations. Innovative artists change these elements for new, surprising sounds that thwart our expectations. Simply changing the rhythm with which the piano accompanies the singer can make a tune sound fresh and exciting. Some listeners will be disappointed when the song doesn't sound the way they've always heard it. Some will be intrigued. How will you feel?

CHAPTER FIVE
ARRANGING

Arranging is the art of changing the music you have before you to make it fresher and more exciting. If you're working as a soloist, accompanying your singing on the piano, you can do this spontaneously during your performance, or you can put thought into it in rehearsal and make your decisions ahead of time. Perhaps you've grown tired of a tune or the way you always play it. Perhaps you want the music to move your audience in a specific, different way. And perhaps you just like to try new things and learn what that brings out in you.

If you're playing with a band, arranging is often a necessary exercise. It's very rare for a band to know the tunes, the style of its repertoire, and its members' abilities and tastes so well that it can get through a gig with no arrangements at all.

Once you've learned a song and are able to play it in the style in which it was written, you may decide that you want to do something more creative with it. This could mean changing anything in a tune: melody, harmony, rhythm, style, tempo, key, form, even the lyrics. You may choose to do some or all of these things in the same song, so that it surprises your audience, you can have more fun with it, and it says something about you that isn't expressed merely by doing the song in the traditional manner. The chart you have in front of you is just a suggestion; you get to make of it what you want to.

STYLE

Jazz players have always taken songs from other sources—Broadway, movies, Tin Pan Alley, folk, and rock 'n' roll artists—and made them jazz by changing things. But you don't have to call your music jazz just because you've changed the original song. If you swing a tune that didn't swing originally, and substitute some jazz chords for the original chords, and improvise over the chords the second time through the form, then it's jazz. But if you change the form and the time signature and a few notes in the melody, it's not necessarily jazz, it's just creative. As always, keep your ears open and you'll hear arrangement ideas that other artists have used to make their interpretations of well-known tunes exciting and fresh.

You already know how to play different rhythms that make a song fit into a particular style. Play the song in each of those styles. Sing over the chords in those new rhythms. How do those new versions feel? Can you use a new style to express something fresh? Would you want to do the entire tune in a different style, or just part of the tune? You may want to start with a Latin rhythm and then go to swing, or vice versa, or back and forth. Maybe you want to change the tune halfway through from a waltz to a jazz waltz. Try it!

KEYS

Play your song in several different keys. Most songs are rangey enough that you'll be able to sing them in only a few keys. But a different key might bring out something new in your voice, or inspire you to sing or play differently. If you can sing the song in more than one key, you may want to put a key change into the song. Most key changes are up a half-step or a whole-step, and rarely up a third. They hardly ever go up any more than that (it would be hard to sing that high), and they almost never go down. A key change can add power, drama, and excitement to a song.

TEMPO

Slow down the tempo or speed it up. You might change an up-tempo number into a ballad. It could make the song seem more serious, or more romantic. You may want to change a ballad into an up-tempo. It can make the song seem more fun, more energetic. Or just a small tempo change may inspire you to play it with a slightly different rhythm, or to sing it differently. You may want to change the tempo halfway through the song, for some variety.

You may also want to play a song using **rubato**. Rubato means that there is no strict sense of tempo, you don't hear even quarter-notes going by, and there is no metronome clicking off beats. You can sing and play the phrases of the music however you like. You can hold notes out as long as you want. You can speed through a phrase, or linger over it. You can switch back and forth between rubato and **strict time**, playing in tempo. Obviously this is a lot easier when it's just you at the piano, because you are in complete control of the tempo. When you're working with others, it can be difficult for everyone to know when to move to the next chord or phrase if there's no steady beat.

FORM

Play around with the form. There's no reason that a song has to begin with a four-bar intro, go through the body of the tune twice, and then end with a four-bar tag. Try a longer intro, or no intro at all. Try going through the tune three times, or only once, or one-and-a-half times. Try starting with the B section. Perhaps a longer tag will give you more time to be creative at the end.

CHORD SUBSTITUTION

Play chords other than the ones you read or hear. This is called **substitution**. It takes a lot of listening and experimenting, but it can lead to more harmonic interest, particularly on tunes that originally had very simple chords.

Although there are several ways to substitute chords, they are all based on the same idea. Certain chords have a role to play in their keys, a function. Any chord that serves the same function as another chord can be substituted for it.

The tonic chord in any key feels like the place to finish a phrase, as though the song had worked its way to a conclusion of some kind, a resolution. Tonic feels like we've come home. Remember, tonic is almost always where the song ends, because music likes to feel finished. Home.

The chord that usually precedes the tonic is the **dominant-seventh chord** (V7). This chord very naturally leads to the tonic. And the leading of the dominant chord to the tonic chord is called **dominant function**. We hear it all the time in every style of music, and have for centuries.

A substitution that pops up over and over again is called **tritone substitution**. The tritone is an unusual interval of three whole-steps, like from C to F-sharp, or from G to C-sharp. So a tritone substitution replaces the original chord with a chord whose root is a tritone away. For instance, in the key of C, the dominant chord G7 would be replaced with D♭7, the chord a tritone away from it.

5-1

This substitution works because the two chords have important things in common. G7 is G-B-D-F, and Db7 is Db-F-Ab-Cb. Cb is enharmonically equivalent to B. So those two chords have two notes in common, F and B. These are the two most senstive, colorful notes in the two chords. (F is 7 in the G7 chord and B is 3, while F is 3 in the Db7 chord and B is 7.) The 3s and the 7s of any chord provide its character, flavor, mood. Also, they are each a half-step away from notes in the C chord. (F is a half-step above E, and B is a half-step below C.) Half-steps have a tendency to pull toward each other, making the chords **resolve**, sound correct together. Play these sets of notes resolving:

5-2

Now put the other notes into the chord and resolve the chords:

 5-3

Can you hear the dominant function in each resolution? Whether you use the G7 or the Db7, the result is the same: C. Home.

Any chord that has enough in common with another chord that it can fulfill its function can be substituted for it. For instance:

 5-4

Those chords are almost exactly alike, and therefore practically interchangeable.

Beyond substitution, you can simply rewrite the harmony to provide more variety and interest. Try things out. How does it sound to sing the melody over the new chords you've tried? New chords may even inspire you to rewrite the melody, or to sing more creatively.

Listen to what others have done, particularly jazz artists. You'll find chord progressions and substitutions you like, and you'll work them into your arrangements. Learn something in one tune, in one key, in one rhythm, and try that new something in another.

Here are two charts, the first with very basic and repetitive chord progressions, and the second with some rewriting:

5-5

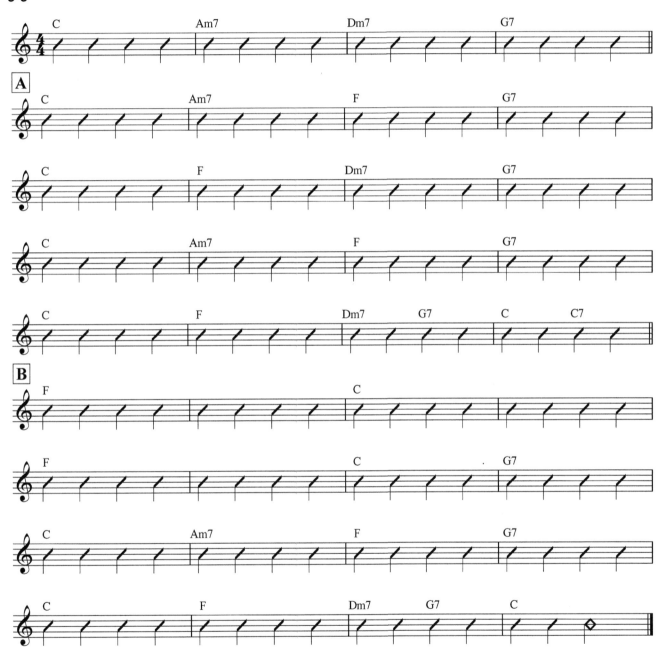

5-6

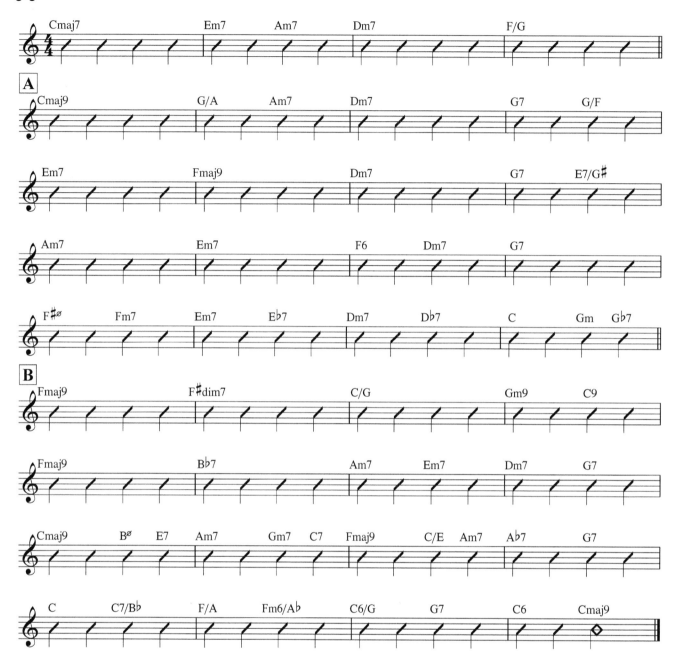

WORKING WITH OTHERS

When writing arrangements, the choice of instruments comes into play. Using additional instruments means working with other players. Now that you know how to accompany yourself, you might wonder what it would be like to work in a group. Your piano playing will have to change a bit, so that it fits with what other musicians are doing.

What will they be doing? That depends on the type of role they play in your band. The **rhythm section** usually accompanies you (the singer). They can take solos while you're not singing, and can work from simple chord charts. They can exist all by themselves.

The rhythm section includes piano (and/or synthesizer), bass (electric or acoustic), drums (and possibly percussion), and maybe guitar.

The bass plays individual notes that establish the rhythm. Since they are often the roots of chords, they define the harmony. In jazz, that might be a walking bass pattern like the ones you've tried in your left-hand piano part. In R&B and rock 'n' roll, it might mean a pattern that repeats often. In ballads, it might mean half-notes and whole-notes.

The drums establish the rhythm even more. Depending on the style of music and the creativity of the drummer, this can be anything from a steady, repetitive, simple pattern (as in a lot of rock 'n' roll) or lots of different rhythms and effects (Latin and jazz). But these last two styles don't have to be complicated. Jazz drummers can "stir soup"— do a soft circular motion with two brushes on a snare drum—or play a basic swing beat on the high hat, and only **fill** from time to time. ("Filling" is playing a more involved pattern for the last bar or so in a section.) Latin music drummers might set a very basic pattern and let the percussion player do the variations, perhaps on congas or bongos.

Guitarists either strum or **chuck**—a detached, rhythmic type of playing—along with the beat, providing harmony in rhythm, or play individual lines, particularly fills, to make the ends of phrases fuller and more interesting.

Synthesizers can also be harmonic, laying down **beds**—whole notes of block harmony—or melodic, playing fills or countermelodies.

Whatever these players choose to play, they should always aim to be supportive of the singer, and stay out of his or her way.

Sidemen are individual instrumentalists: trumpet, trombone, saxophone, clarinet, even guitar, who might play very little while you're singing (to stay out of your way) and then take solos when you stop.

Sections are groups of players—brass, woodwinds, strings—who are there to provide a fuller sound, more texture, more melodic and harmonic interest, and perhaps to provide lusher, more dramatic solos. Sections should always have well-thought-out arrangements, and not be expected to create something from a chord chart.

Where do you fit into all of this? The good news is, you can do a lot less, because so much of what you needed to do when you were by yourself is being done by others.

You can just play chords, in both hands or just one hand, because your left hand doesn't have to play the bass part anymore. In fact, it shouldn't, because it will inevitably clash with what the bass player is doing. Your playing can be fuller and more rhythmic. You can concentrate on melody lines and fills, and take solos when you're not singing, and not have to worry about providing all the harmony and rhythm while you do.

Again, if you don't coordinate what you're playing with the other musicians, there can be clashes. Too much might be going on to serve you, the singer. That's why playing in a band can be tricky if someone doesn't know what he is doing. Bands often have more than just chord charts. They have arrangements with notes on staves so that all the instruments will have specific parts to play that will work well together. And they rehearse often enough to know what each player is going to play, and how to stay out of each other's way. The more instruments you have in a band, the more important it is to know what everyone is called on to do. Fortunately, that probably means that you don't have to do a lot at the piano. In this case, less is more.

But because a good band gives everyone a chance to shine, you may still be called on to take your turn as the featured performer. The skill you develop from playing solo will help you when your band shines the spotlight on you.

Playing with others can be an exciting challenge, inspiring you to play familiar tunes in different ways. That can make it fun and unpredictable for you, and keep the magic of music from waning. Other musicians will also inspire you with their creativity.

CHAP WRAP

If a professional arranger is asked to chart a song for a swing band, an R&B artist, or a Latin orchestra, he knows what elements to use so that the harmony and rhythm supporting the melody sound appropriate for that style. But if he has the opportunity to be more creative, he can change elements halfway through the song, or substitute new ones completely. If you're in a band, you'll have to work through new arrangement ideas with your colleagues, and come to a group decision. But as a solo artist, you will have complete control of your music, and can change any element of it that you want at any time. Changing things should inspire you to sing more creatively, and perhaps more emotionally as well. Try as many different things with your music as you can, because you never know what will make a song more exciting and personal for you, and what will make it moving for your audience.

CONCLUSION

You've learned how to play melodies, at least well enough to plunk out tunes that you've never heard before. You've learned how to play chords to accompany the melody, one way if you're playing it, another if you're singing it. And you've learned how to play those chords, either from charts that already exist or from ones you write yourself, in various styles. Finally, you've learned how to arrange those songs so that they are expressive and creative. If you feel you need more practice reading music, hearing chords, understanding theory, or transposing and transcribing, my first two books, *Musicianship for Singers* and *Teach Yourself to Read Music,* provide more explanations, examples, and exercises.

I hope that along the way you've learned a bit about how music does what it does. Music is a huge world, and much has been written about the effect it can have on us, particularly on our emotions. Composers and arrangers know what chords and intervals and rhythms usually sound happy or sad or angry or scary or funny. They know how to manipulate those elements so their music can make us feel those things, in the movie theatre, on a recording, or at a live concert.

When you play through these songs, do you hear things that provoke certain emotions? Are there certain chords that thrill you? Do melodies have notes in them, or intervals, that bring you to tears? Rhythms that make you want to get up and dance? Notice them. Much of music, just like the other art forms, is about setting up expectations, and then either fulfilling them or breaking them. How do you feel when you expect to hear something, and the composer comes up with something else? And how do you feel when the music does exactly what you expected it to do?

I have never wanted to reinforce the musical stereotypes that we hear in music all the time: bouncy major key music = happy, slow minor key music = sad. Many tests have been done to show how listeners of different backgrounds can feel the same things about pieces of music, because of these stereotypical elements. Personally, I don't think stereotypes are good for music, and there is no reason why major music has to be happy and minor music has to be sad. But you are the artist, you get to make the decisions. Do you want to your music to affect the audience in a predictable manner, or do you want to explore different paths?

Try as many things with your songs as you can, listen hard and evaluate. Then make the decisions you make because you want to communicate with your audience, and you know how to use the elements of music to do so.

Finally, since you're a vocalist, sing as creatively as possible. Now that you know what scales and chords and rhythms are, you won't feel lost when you try to improvise vocally, or change things in the music. There is a lot to say about vocal interpretation, particularly melodic improvisation and scat when you're singing jazz. But knowing what key you're in, knowing what notes are in the scale associated with that key, knowing a maj7 chord from a min9 chord—all this will help you to hear more things, identify what you hear, sing them back, and create new things with your vocal interpretation. And when you listen to other musicians, you can say things like "I really liked the way he went from Latin to Swing in that tune," or "I would never have thought of using that chord progression there," or "What a wonderful ending she tacked onto that song," or "Listen to the huge interval he finishes that phrase with!" That should inspire you to find your own ways to make your audience respond. And that's your ultimate goal: to express yourself to an audience and get them to respond to you. Good luck.

ANSWERS

CHAPTER TWO

2-4(A)

2-9(A)

2-15(A)

2-17(A)

2-18(A)

CHAPTER THREE

3-6(A)

3-10(A)

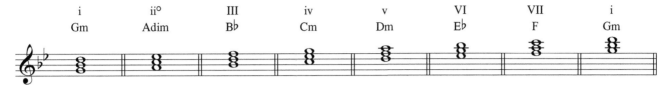

3-11(A)

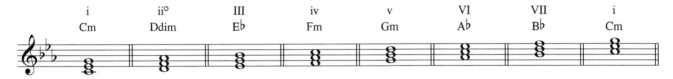

3-13(A)

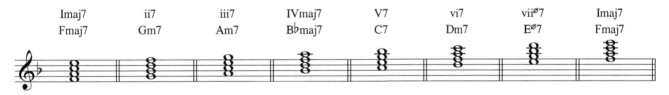

3-14(A)

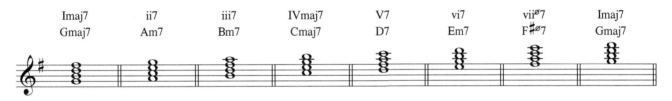

3-15(A)

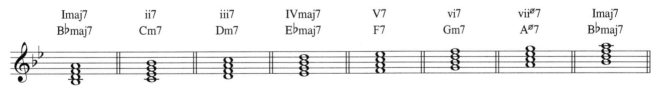

3-16(A)

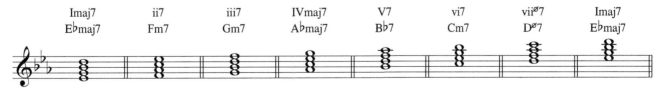

3-17(A)

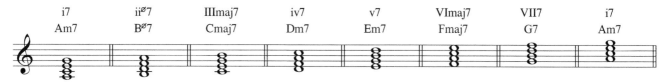

i7	ii⌀7	IIImaj7	iv7	v7	VImaj7	VII7	i7
Am7	B⌀7	Cmaj7	Dm7	Em7	Fmaj7	G7	Am7

3-22(A)

	(G°7)			(D°7)	
D+	Gdim7	Esus	B♭+	Ddim7	Asus

3-24(A)

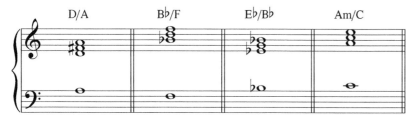

D/A   B♭/F   E♭/B♭   Am/C

3-29(A)

B♭maj7/D   D7/A   E♭maj7/D   E♭maj9/G   Gmaj9/D   E♭9/F

3-31(A)

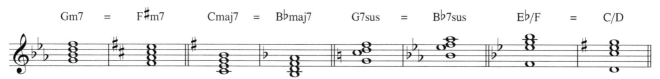

Gm7 = F♯m7   Cmaj7 = B♭maj7   G7sus = B♭7sus   E♭/F = C/D

3-33(A)

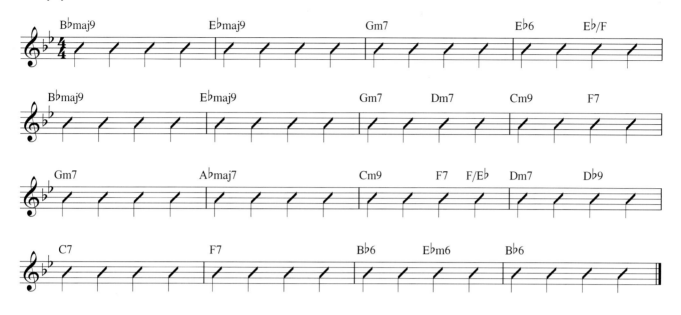

3-36(A)

3-37(A)

3-38(A)

3-39(A)

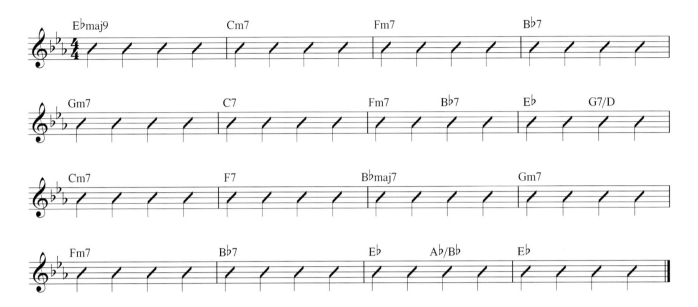

ABOUT THE AUTHOR

Jeffrey Deutsch has sung onstage—in nightclubs and ballrooms, in concert halls and sports arenas—for over 40 years. From main stage shows for corporate and private parties, to swing music in front of a big band in a ballroom for a large audience of dancers, to jazz on the world's most luxurious cruise ships for intimate late night crowds, Jeffrey brings energy, humor, sophistication, and love for great music and performing to everything he does.

In addition to private teaching, Jeffrey has taught jazz, pop, and rock vocals at Elmhurst College in Elmhurst, Illinois, and in Chicago at Columbia College and at the Center for Voice. He has been a vocal coach, helping students put shows together, and has taught classes in chart-writing and sight-singing. He has given lessons in piano accompaniment, based on his many years of playing for himself onstage and in piano bars.

Jeffrey is the author of two books that have helped singers develop practical skills, *Musicianship for Singers* and *Teach Yourself to Read Music*, both distributed by Hal Leonard.

Special Thanks
This book is dedicated to Dr. John Jeffrey and Mary Stewart,
both of whom have helped me in many ways over many years.